KIDS IN HISTORY

How Did Kids Live During the Civil War?

BY

Gareth Stevens PUBLISHING

Please visit our website, www.garethstevens.com. For a free color catalog of all our high-quality books, call toll free 1-800-542-2595 or fax 1-877-542-2596.

Library of Congress Cataloging-in-Publication Data

Names: Quick, Megan, author.
Title: How did kids live during the Civil War? / Megan Quick.
Description: Buffalo, New York : Gareth Stevens Publishing, [2024] | Series: Kids in history | Includes bibliographical references and index.
Identifiers: LCCN 2023008337 | ISBN 9781538288108 (library binding) | ISBN 9781538288092 (paperback) | ISBN 9781538288115 (ebook)
Subjects: LCSH: United States–History–Civil War, 1861-1865–Children–Juvenile literature. | Children and war–United States–History–19th century–Juvenile literature. | United States–History–Civil War, 1861-1865–Participation, Juvenile–Juvenile literature.
Classification: LCC E540.C47 Q53 2024 | DDC 973.7/083–dc23/eng/20230222
LC record available at https://lccn.loc.gov/2023008337

Portions of this work were originally authored by Sarah Machajewski and published as *A Kid's Life During the American Civil War*. All new material in this edition was authored by Megan Quick.

Published in 2024 by
Gareth Stevens Publishing
2544 Clinton Street
Buffalo, NY 14224

Designer: Jen Schoembs
Editor: Megan Quick

Photo credits: Cover (house and cannons), p. 1 (house and cannons) Zack Frank/Shutterstock.com; cover (boy), p. 1 (boy) Krakenimages.com/Shutterstock.com; cover (background), p.1 (background), series art (background) Login/Shutterstock.com; pp. 5, 21 North Wind Picture Archives/Alamy.com; p. 6 muratart/Shutterstock.com; p. 7 Everett Collection/Shutterstock.com; p. 9 (inset) Strobridge & Co. Lith/loc.gov; p. 9 (main) THEPALMER/iStock.com; p. 11 Stephens, H. L. (Henry Louis)/loc.gov; pp. 13, 19 courtesy of Library of Congress; p. 15 Campwillowlake/iStock.com; p. 17 Artepics/Alamy.com.

Printed in the United States of America

CPSIA compliance information: Batch #CS24GS: For further information contact Gareth Stevens at 1-800-542-2595.

Contents

Words in the glossary appear in **bold** type the first time they are used in the text.

A Different Time

You may have learned about the American Civil War in school. In the 1860s, the country was **divided:** North against South. Your teacher likely told you about important leaders and soldiers. But what about the kids?

Children at that time had no TV or computers. They received letters instead of email. And with many adults away fighting, life was hard: more chores, less food, and many worries. Let's find out more about why the Civil War happened and what it was like to be a kid at that time.

A family says goodbye to a soldier. More than 3 million Americans fought in the Civil War.

Life in the Past

Big families were very common at the time of the Civil War. The average family had at least five children.

Fields and Farms

cotton

The Civil War began on April 12, 1861. At that time, most of the South was **rural**. There were many farms of all sizes. Very big farms were called plantations. Growing and selling crops such as cotton and **tobacco** was important business in the South.

Running a plantation was hard work. **Enslaved** Africans did most of that work. White enslavers forced them to work without pay. They treated enslaved people as if they were property. The plantation owners made lots of money since they didn't pay the enslaved Africans.

Life in the Past

Plantation owners put the children of enslaved people to work at a very young age. These enslavers often took the children away from their families and sold them to other plantations.

This family of enslaved people in South Carolina included five **generations**.

Cities and Factories

Life was very different in the North. More people lived in cities and towns. Machines in factories made work faster and easier. There were also many more railroads in the North. These were helpful in moving goods and people quickly.

The Black population in the North was fairly small, but most were free. They joined other Northerners who wanted enslavement to end. The South didn't want this. President Abraham Lincoln tried to keep the country together. But the two sides broke apart and the war began.

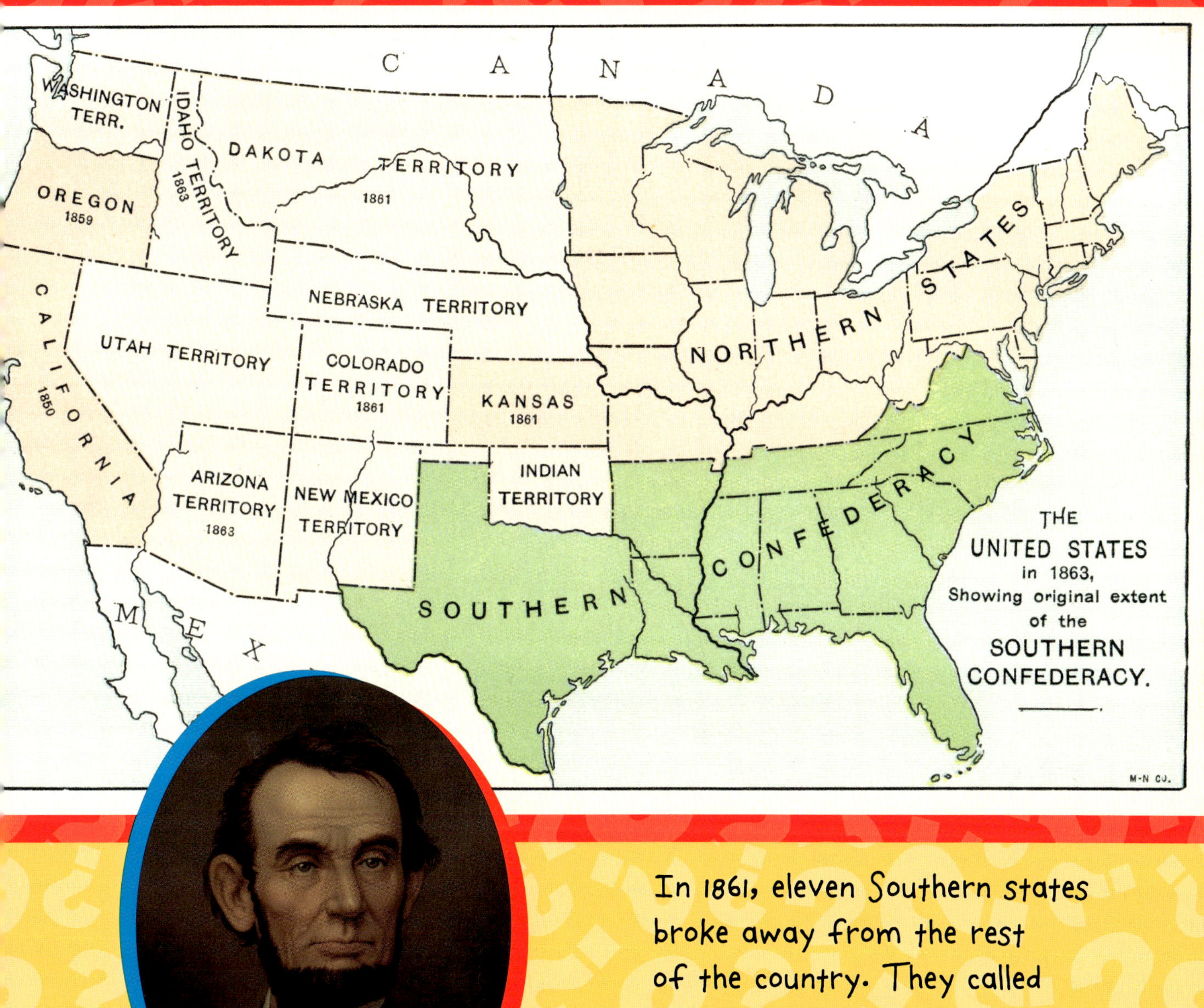

President Abraham Lincoln

In 1861, eleven Southern states broke away from the rest of the country. They called themselves the Confederacy. The rest of the United States was called the Union.

Going Hungry

At first, the war was exciting for children. They enjoyed watching military parades and soldiers marching in uniform. But as the war went on, food prices rose. Fighting destroyed farms. Some armies stole food from homes to feed their soldiers. Families didn't have enough to eat.

The problem was worse in the South, where most of the battles took place. People couldn't find necessary food items such as flour, sugar, and meat. Many children lived off small amounts of plain food such as rice or corn.

Some families had to leave their homes when there wasn't enough food. There were special camps for **refugees** during the war.

Hard Times

With many fathers and brothers away at war, children had to do the work men usually did. On farms, they worked in the fields, chopped wood, and took care of animals. In homes, children cooked, sewed, and took care of younger brothers and sisters.

Kids also had to make do with their clothing. Cloth was hard to find, so families patched up old clothes. For boys, this was knickers, or short pants, with **suspenders** and loose shirts. Girls wore dresses much like the ones their mothers wore.

Life in the Past

Many older boys and girls took jobs working in factories that made guns and other tools for war.

One of the hardest things about the war was worrying about loved ones. This little girl holds a picture of her father, who died in battle.

School Struggles

Children often had to leave school to stay home and help their families. Some tried to keep up with their studies by learning at home. In the South, many schools closed completely during the war.

For those who could attend, school was very different than it is now. It was often a one-room schoolhouse, with many ages learning together. Students worked on reading, writing, and math. They might sing war songs during morning lessons. It was a way to support the war and the soldiers who were away fighting.

Life in the Past

Enslavers didn't allow Black boys and girls to attend school. A few brave teachers taught enslaved children in secret. If they were caught, both the student and teacher would be **punished**.

At the time of the war, many children were finished with school as early as age 12.

Fun and Games

Most children didn't have much free time during the war. But when they were able, kids might go fishing or play outside. Their games often had to do with war. Playing soldiers was a favorite activity for boys. Girls pretended to be nurses helping the wounded troops.

Children also enjoyed reading. In the North, where supplies were easier to get, magazines were popular. Some favorites were *Our Young Folks* and *The Little Pilgrim.* They included articles, stories, plays, and poems—many having to do with the war.

Life in the Past

Writing and receiving letters was an important part of daily life during the war. Soldiers wrote about battles and how they felt. Families wrote to tell the soldiers about life at home.

A mother reads about the war in the newspaper while her children march about like soldiers.

The Smallest Soldiers

While most children did their part by helping at home, a few joined the war. Some children carried messages for the troops. Others became **musicians**, such as drummers, who marched along with the soldiers. They weren't supposed to fight, but they were often in danger, and some were hurt or killed.

Twelve-year-old Johnny Clem was a drummer for the Union army. In September 1863, the Battle of Chickamauga broke out in Georgia, and Johnny shot a Confederate officer. He became a hero for the Union.

Johnny Clem was wounded twice in the war. He left the army at age 13 but rejoined several years later.

Life in the Past

Soldiers in the Union army were supposed to be at least 18 years old. There was no age requirement for the Confederate army. Both sides needed soldiers badly, so they often accepted boys as young as 13.

Peace at Last

After four long years, the Civil War ended in April 1865. The North **celebrated** its success, while much of the South was destroyed. Newly freed Black people were hopeful that their lives would improve. They began looking for jobs and education.

Most children were glad the war was over. They waited for their fathers and brothers to come home. Some soldiers came back wounded and others didn't make it home at all. The country needed a long time to heal, but it was **united** once again.

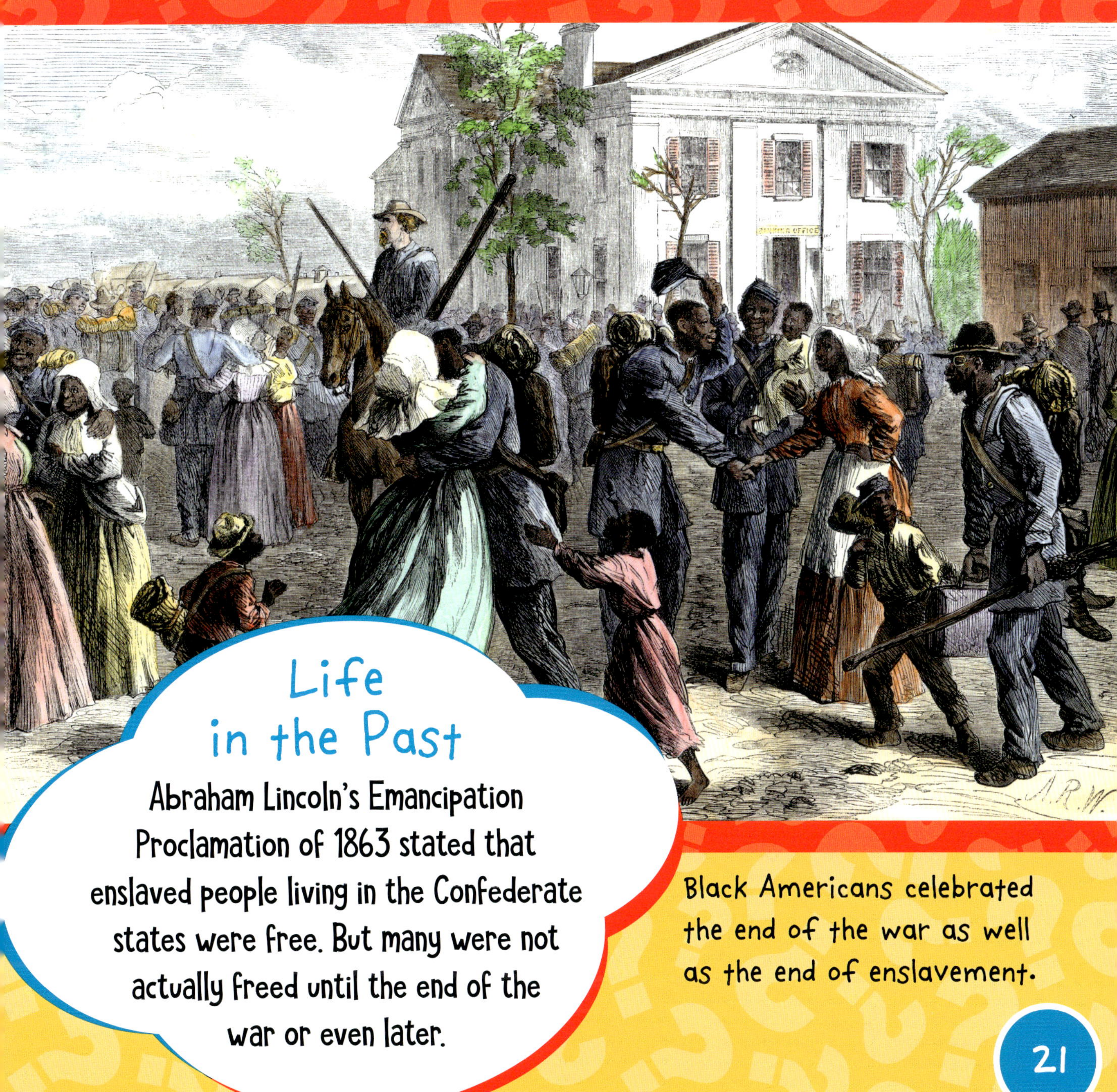

Life in the Past

Abraham Lincoln's Emancipation Proclamation of 1863 stated that enslaved people living in the Confederate states were free. But many were not actually freed until the end of the war or even later.

Black Americans celebrated the end of the war as well as the end of enslavement.

Glossary

celebrate: To honor with special activities.

divide: To break up.

enslavement: Having to do with being owned by another person and forced to work without pay.

generation: A group of individuals born about the same time.

musician: One who plays, makes, or sings music.

punish: To make someone suffer for wrongdoing.

refugee: Someone who is seeking a safe place to live, especially during a time of war.

rural: Having to do with the countryside.

suspenders: Bands worn over the shoulders to hold up pants.

tobacco: A mainly American plant that has sticky leaves and tube-shaped flowers.

united: The state of being joined together for a common purpose.

For More Information

Books

Katz, Susan B. *The History of the Civil War: A History Book for New Readers*. Emeryville, CA: Rockridge Press, 2021.

Messner, Kate. *History Smashers: The Underground Railroad*. New York, NY: Random House Books for Young Readers, 2022.

Patrick, Denise Lewis. *If You Lived During the Civil War*. New York, NY: Scholastic, 2022.

Websites

DK Find Out!: American Civil War
www.dkfindout.com/us/history/american-civil-war/
Learn more about important people, places, and events of the Civil War.

Ducksters: Children During the Civil War
www.nps.gov/subjects/undergroundrailroad/upload/Junior-Ranger-Activity-Booklet.pdf
Find out more about how kids got involved in the war.

National Park Service
www.nps.gov/subjects/undergroundrailroad/upload/Junior-Ranger-Activity-Booklet.pdf
Explore the hard road to freedom for enslaved people in the 1800s.

Publisher's note to educators and parents: Our editors have carefully reviewed these websites to ensure that they are suitable for students. Many websites change frequently, however, and we cannot guarantee that a site's future contents will continue to meet our high standards of quality and educational value. Be advised that students should be closely supervised whenever they access the internet.

Index